Magic

Gloucestershire Poetry Society
Anthology
2019

Black Eyes Publishing UK

Magic - Gloucestershire Poetry Society Anthology 2019
© Peter Lay 2019

Published by Black Eyes Publishing UK, 2019
Brockworth, Gloucestershire, England
www.blackeyespublishinguk.co.uk

ISBN: 978-1-913195-07-6

All poems in this anthology remain within the copyright of the individual poets. They have asserted their moral right under the Copyright, Designs and Patents Act, 1988, to be identified as the authors of their work.

All Rights reserved. No part of this publication may be reproduced, copied, stored in a retrieval system, or transmitted, in any form or by any means, without the prior written consent of the copyright holder(s), nor be otherwise circulated in any form of binding or cover other than that in which it is published and without a similar condition being imposed on the subsequent purchaser.

A CIP catalogue record for this title is available from the British Library.

Cover design: Jason Conway, cre8urbrand.
                  www.cre8urbrand.co.uk

Poetry edits: Z D Dicks

GPS Waterstones Gloucester

Magic

Contents

9   Introduction

11 Mind Magic ~ Josephine Lay
12 Magic for a Hungry Child ~ Maria Castro Dominguez
13 Magic ~ Z D Dicks
14 Initiation ~ Laura Theis
16 The Night I Met a Mermaid ~ Carol Sheppard
18 love potion ~ Sue Johnson
19 Where the Magic Lives ~ Sue Kinsella
20 Incantation for Ellen Hayward ~ JLM Morton
22 So You Want to Burn a Witch? ~ Tessa Foley
24 Bioluminescence ~ Miriam Calleja
25 'Magic' ~ Emily Hall
26 Here comes The Moles ~ Susie Wilson
28 Witches' Exhibition ~ Patricia M Osborne
29 Magical Creatures ~ Sue Kinsella
30 Misrepresentation ~ Clive Oseman
32 the herbalist ~ Josephine Lay
33 Magic ~ Chris Barber
34 Boots Magic ~ Peter Lay
36 Eleven Floating Thoughts ~ Jason Conway
38 Towel Poem ~ Aiden Baker
39 Part Trick ~ Charlie Markwick
40 Her Alchemy ~ Tish Camp
41 Eventide ~ Kayleigh Campbell

43 Contributors

55 Thanks
57 Finally

59 Gloucester Poetry Festival 2019

This year has been a very busy one for many of the poets of The Gloucestershire Poetry Society with many having their work published in journals, anthologies and collections. This feels fitting as the theme of our poetry this year has been 'magic' and it certainly feels that we have been under a spell. I personally have heard the comments regarding our continued efforts to promote poetry for all. The work herein is a collection of poems collated from a pool of poets of all levels and backgrounds. A collection I hope you enjoy, as much as the poets themselves as they crafted their work,
Yours in the art,

Z D Dicks

(Ziggy)

Josephine Lay

Mind Magic

I weave poetic spells in lines of verse
that slide haunting visions into minds
I lighten verbs   choose weightless nouns
that float fluently on breaths of thought
Earth's gravity holds us captive
against a solid ground…
But mind should float in sunbeams
rush recklessly with rapids
spread like waves on sand
under the moon's influence

Like a cauldron   an anthology
should be full of magic incantations
filtered through phrases and stirred
by inspiration   words are the herbs
hand-picked under a gibbous moon
sprinkled to enhance enchantment
the potion   dispensed with gentle voice
adds suffering or joy to those that taste
imprisoned in dreams   they implore blessing
seek to placate me   like a goddess

I am deaf to any supplication
my poetry pours into lithe minds
poignant visions of my perception
this mystical invocation…
That mind should float in sunbeams
rush recklessly with rapids
spread like lace on the sands
beneath the moon's incandescence

María Castro Domínguez

Magic for a Hungry Child

I filled you
with sun,
mammatus clouds
flower carpets
gargles of chirps,
peacock feathers
and azure rich fishes.
I fed you cotton-
candied katsuras,
a million cloves from
the Maluku Isles,
gallons of Columbian coffee,
Oolong tea leaves,
Peruvian goat's milk
so white and heavy
your eyes were filled
with light.
I tried to feed you
a mirror to deflect
all that's outside
in you, but you growled
and showed me your gums.
I even tried
the moon,
the stars,
and finally the whole
firmament,
but you cried and cried
still hungry,
your mouth open wide.

Z D Dicks

Magic

In the lounge   the soft huff
of breath   is like a cloud surfing
and a half moaned dream
an aeroplane   on its way to a holiday
my head semi pressed   to cushion
feet   slippered   in warm sand

Silence fizzles   and static bubbles
stirs me   from a mid day snooze
with no alarm set   crackles in lifted
ears   waiting   nose is tuned to station
bbq sauce   smouldering on bacon
meat wafted   on short wave

In front   on mantlepiece   cross
legged   brought back from dead
a wooden Amida buddha smirks
under carved closed eyes   an origami
butterfly   rests in open palm   gifted
by a monk   next to hand drawn crow

A card   crafted by an infant   waves
in a draught   I yawn a smile   fully
awake in a dream

Laura Theis

Initiation

It starts with an apple -
not poisoned, nothing so ordinary.
Just a round ruddy marvel grown from bitter
seeds – the lush daughter of time and the patience
of trees.

Pick the apple that calls to you. You cannot go wrong.
She will have picked you in her turn. Hold her
close to your face. Seek your own
reflection in her red. Bite down. Isolate
the edge of her acerbity from the sweetness until you find
the sting: a sour prickle, but not unpleasant.
Swallow.

Now let the wish rise. You thought you knew it, you don't.
You thought it was yours, yet you'd never understood that you'd
been sheltering
such yearning, unfamiliar in its sudden force.
Let it fill you, but don't hold it, let it go without speaking.
Unleash it with a quiet breath, palms open.
(You will need to uncurl your fists for this.)

What leaves you is more than a wind storm or even a creature.
It is something you made but cannot comprehend.
When you have recovered from the shock,
the frightening jolt and scope of your power,
you coil back into yourself, stilled.
Like the quiet mother of a wilful child you watch it whirl and rage
and tear
at the fabric of the world.

You stand there as a sapling might, calm
within your new-found emptiness,
and tell yourself the unfamiliar truth
that you are ready –

Carol Sheppard

The Night I Met a Mermaid

That night, I found a mermaid
at the bottom of my third pink gin
amongst lumped ice and juniper berries
lazily swimming on her back, circling the glass bowl.

>She grabbed my hands and dragged me under.
>We swam, our bodies, skin to scales.
>She took my face in her hands,
>kissed me hard;
>Chilled salt lips, so soft;
>her hair, ribbons of seaweed, caressed me,
>tail wrapped tightly round my legs.
>She pulled back, laughed at my expression,
>sea-green eyes searched mine,
>brows arched,
>flicked her shimmering tail.

She wanted to take me deeper,
where light fades to darkness,
to a trench that night creatures prowl and
sea cucumbers writhe under jellyfish glow.
I imagined spider crabs with gigantic stone legs,
toxic breathing tube worms,
viperfish with sharp spiny teeth and deadly eel-like frilled sharks all
jostling and fighting in the gloom around
rusty barnacled wrecks.

>I gasped, struggled for surface;
>gulped great lungfuls of sweet air.

When I turned around
               she was gone
the sting of her kiss still on my lips.

Sue Johnson

love potion

there was no time to close the curtains
the universe had shrunk to just the two of them

they unpeeled each other's clothing
discovering magic at each unveiling

frost sparkled on the pavements far below
stars gleamed sharp as tin outside the window

street sounds faded away like smoke
there was only the music of their hearts

the touch of skin on skin in the attic room
where passion spiralled light years away

when they finally came together she noticed
the explosion of colours in her head

different from anything she had seen before
a flickering of pink, white, ice blue and silver

against a background of indigo blue
and then after the climax deep foxglove pink

Sue Kinsella

Where the Magic Lives

On a tilt, a spin
In the circle
Of pupil
Blue of iris -
Clip of heel
Crease of jean
Pull of belt
Cling of shirt
Curve of shoulder -
Bell of glasses
- back door step
Tune of adult and child
Beauty of the human image
Nature of silence -
The day we met.

JLM Morton

Incantation for Ellen Hayward

Let Ellen Hayward be not delivered on this implacable plaque of law and local history, pinned by ink pens through the groin, gut and gallery to Hansard, and say these words three times:
>This as my remedy for the malediction of my tongue.
>This as my remedy for influenza, for the foregone fifty pounds of a farmer, a fence-maker and a father feared insane.
>This as my remedy for fucking men until their hair grows back.

And when Old Ellen's in the dock, she will levitate over Cinderford and say:
>I am condemned to the bad renditions of a toy box theatre,
>To the repellents of cold iron, hazel sticks, salt circles and the cockerel's crow,
>To abide the hacking away of my hands for their healing powers.

And when Ellen perceives the pull of thirty witnesses in her defence, she will say:
>All this is conjecture.

Let her say I am orchids, I am grizzled skipper, wild sow, spleenwort, moonlight, I am an abnormal condition. I treat the knees of Cheltenham servant girls for nothing, for everything:
>Permit me the trade.
>This black lock and this stone of grief.

Let her who could not save her third born from the workhouse feed on wet nurse milk with her own mouth, spit it in St Anthony's

source, scoop up whiteish well water, swallow all; then say:
> Take down your horseshoes and your hawthorn, 'I am only another of my unfortunate sex – human.'
> And at last I may go home.

Then will Ellen Hayward retreat where none can see her, salved by cooling limestone, forest mulch and coal, buried alive as her daughter's bones.

Note: Ellen Hayward was a herbalist and phrenologist, the last person charged with witchcraft in Gloucestershire, at Littledean Courthouse, 1906. The phrase 'I am only another of my unfortunate sex – human,' is Ellen Hayward's own, from her statement to police.

Tessa Foley

So You Want to Burn a Witch?

No housebound? No issue?
Past her fortieth year?
Why not smear badger blood
On the shop display panes?
Stain the doormat with paint.

Plumb the dirtiest pool
For your thoughts on the women
Your own ducking stool,
Smoke out all the power
That lies in the womb.

The century twentieth-first
And foremost, your custom desire
Is a rare, bloody stake
And to take that time back
To when Agnes S could've been
Yours to break.

Scared of the strong, of the skyclad
Their charge?
And their faith in their arms,
Spit while they're distilling
Their truths into jars or

The stars that they've plucked
Just to make something new,
It's you who wants to birth the harm,
The taste of ashes on your tongue
And in your lungs that crawling hate
Mundane, you were born too late.

An unconditioned, tortured girl,
A girl who cooks,
Alongside her, you will burn the books,
The pent up scorn
To spend your lives
"Stop scrying – get on, make good wives!"

But string of women
Holding own
How lonely it must make you feel,
There standing tall on College Street
That magick wall,
You cannot, cannot burn us all.

Miriam Calleja

Bioluminescence

A poem exists in your face. You lift your gaze to devour everything that's in front of you. A gentleness descends, it reminds you that we are strangers. I rest my cold forehead on your back; the transition is smooth and absorbs ink. You laugh at the noise it makes. Now, letters fall into my wide open jaw. Chewing in silence, I show you that I understand.

Emily Hall (aged 9)

'Magic'

I know there's no such thing as magic
But as magical as my life might seem
To be a witch or a sorcerer
Has been my only dream

I'd rather have a magic wand
Than any other thing
I prefer to have invisible cloaks
Than a priceless diamond ring

I would ride a broomstick
And soar up to the sky
Or ride on a dragons back
And together we would fly

There is no such thing as magic
But I will always believe
That it's waiting for me somewhere
A task for me to achieve

Susie Wilson

Here Come The Moles

Once a month the sun
aligns with the moon, to
drop a total dark over
church yards and car parks.

After evensong, the priest
and all the congregation
gone, the darkness deepens.
Then, the moles will come.

Close your eyes and look!
Moles who know the groom,
to the left. Family and friends
of the mole-bride, on the right.

Mole nose-whiskers, twitch
your neighbours into sight.
Give and take the peace of
mammal greetings.

Everyone here is unified
in black, grey claws, red eyes.
No lights, no need. No moon
and no-one minds.

The only white, the church's
thick stone hide. Instead
all inner hollows dim, like soil
pushed up from underground.

Undivided now, still small moles
await in velvet silence.
'Dearly beloved.
We have gathered ourselves.'

Patricia M Osborne

Witches' Exhibition

Witch beads, symbols of service,
hang below their breasts, a string
of clear and coloured blobs simulate
a *Rosary* without the cross.

We shiver at hag stones,
blues, whites, rusted reds,
rough, smooth, uneven forms
and shapes with holes
like doughnuts.

Small grainy pebbles,
swollen mounds of sand,
starfish like imprints
carved into fairy crowns.

Tista Phista Sistra...

thout—
 tout...

spells weave in and out—

We each write down, half of the charms
to pass to one another sometime, later on...

Heeding the warning...
 we peel the papers away...

keep the words of the curses firmly apart
 to ensure the enchantments never entwine.

Sue Kinsella

Magical Creatures

Tuesday last I considered a life force at buzz
airborne above white bread in spread mode;
black, size- pinhead.
What creature is this? I asked.
What name frames its beginning and end?
Is this all brain and what of intelligent order in flight?
Out maneuvered in my own kitchen –
Dishcloth in left hand whip flicked whistles
while a stainless steel knife stabbed pointless at air.
When my foe vanished (more than ten attempts did not land a strike)
I disengaged. Soaked up the scene; not in angst more in
cheerful ecstasy at our weird artistic dance.
Invisible forms in silent adulation at this
once in a lifetime performance came alive -
revealed in terrestrial colours. We mimed in miniature -
winked with both eyes, high fived and blew kisses;
Boundless in childish bliss - I allowed myself remember
how good that felt.

Clive Oseman

Misrepresentation

Magic is real, I'm told.
You can see it unfold
if you know what to look for
if you channel your thoughts
to the wavelength you ought to.

It's not a phenomenon that's new
it's existed through the ages
runs right through the pages of history
but to me, remains a mystery.

It isn't Paul Daniels or Dynamo.
When illusionists catch the eye,
you know they look better than reality,
that if you saw them with clarity
there's nothing special in their feats,
just deceit and suspension of disbelief.

It isn't the world of wizards and witches,
good versus evil and a child's upheaval
as portrayed in the barely believable tales
of the boy who lived,
the golden gift to the silver screen
where every supposedly suspense filled scene
led to a climax that all fans had foreseen.

The good guy won.
Because that's how it's done, right?
That's the magic of movies for sure.
We all go home cured of the blues
safe in the knowledge that good guys don't lose.

Magic powers like those found in fiction
or perfect performance by people
who have practiced for hours
misrepresent the meaning of the word.

It is simpler than that.
It is love and respect
reflected in actions of those we care for,
those we select to share life with
and the special bond of families.
The joy of living to bring up our kids.

I cannot confirm that it really exists.

Josephine Lay

the herbalist

fragrance leads her to each scented plant
growing beneath the inky Cyprus trees
whose branches sieve the scattered stars

her hands glint in the luminescence
fingers stroke the fronds as she picks
aromatic leaves from each fragile stem

placing them like precious jewels in
the depths of the black bag tied at her waist
her long skirt brushes the grass as she

collects her bounty of herbs   at length
she stands tall   moonlight painting highlights
on her cheeks   eyes closed   she communes

becomes one with trees   senses a zephyr
rustle her dress as though she had leaves
believes she might stay like this eternally

but the moon pales behind light cloud
halos out its radiance   ripples light
Circe flows beneath its influence

Chris Barber

Magic

You won't find it up there, on a stage,
no street vendor, conjuring for the telly,
away from the glitz and glamour, no
suspended superstar in cube of glass.
That's entertainment.

This is life.

There's magic in your lovers eyes,
in the beauty of a baby's cry. In
the magnificence of the natural world,
where all that glitters can be seen as gold.

Magical human endeavour.

A Bolt sprint, a Comaneci perfect ten.
Maradona from his own half, a poet's pen,
a Da Vinci study part art, part science,
handily invented household appliance.

Look around.

There's magic in the everyday,
so much beauty seen as ordinary.
Charlie's theory or divine plan,
so much more than sleight of hand.

Peter Lay

Boots Magic

In a Wiltshire field
Not far from Avebury…
Is buried a boot
Well two boots actually
Two red boots
Dr Martens

Under the turf they lie
Deep in the earth…
Buried
Down deep… watered
As the rain falls…

We were walking
across Charles Bridge
in Prague, she said
When you've finished
with those boots
can I have them?
I looked at her, *Why?*
And she sang,
Nai nana nai

We walked around
the stone circle at Avebury
in the dark of night
Her dress floating sensually
in the breeze I looked at her
Why? And she sang,
Nai nana nai

In a Wiltshire field
Not far from Avebury…
Is buried a boot
Well two boots actually
Two red boots
Dr Martens

Under the turf they lie
Deep in the earth
Buried… down deep
Watered
As the rain falls…

Jason Conway

Eleven Floating Thoughts

6:48
Four rubber spinning discs are sliced to air
as they leave solid ground
dissecting zephyr's as they raise sky bound

6:49
Sets of eardrums pop from rising pressure
like submariners, as gravity bears down
bags of sweets are polished

6:50
Wandering thoughts drift
to a myriad of aspirations and night dreams
in glazed stares through misted glass ovals

6:51
A magic ship ferries expectant travellers
and their baggage, sharing stale air
and cramped legroom

6:52
Shimmering specks of light dance
through cold looking glasses
like glittering spells sending minds into fantasy

6:53
Two giant steel fins trail vapour waves
surfing vapoured currents
metal swells disappear into the dark expanse

6:54
Windows reflect charcoal and blue
tired faces, bathers in a midnight lake
in their lanes of polished crystal

6:55
A cargo of bottled dreams bobs
afloat in a cloudless black void
like messages, in sealed containers

6:56
This dark gently stalls, juddering
employment thoughts, hurrying to rare pause
where jet engines stroke a misted sphere

6:57
Hearts beat like sunken drums,
Hit by rushing streams as heavy lids
fall shut, at change of pressure

6:58
Wings spread blackened air
as wands circling a cauldron
a call for sleeping minds to wake
in sunshine and warmer climbs

Aidan Baker

Towel Poem

Unexpectedly
a towel slips from its rail
like a decided
human, or (do they decide
in that way?) a dog or cat.

I'd rather not see
the towel get up again.
Shades of M.R. James.
A serious fright partly
because it never happens.

The opposite scare:
someone moves decisively
but then does not move
and still remains unmoving
and still remains unmoving

Charlie Markwick

Party Trick

"Look" he said "it's magic."
"No" she thought, "it's tragic."
That early alchemy of love was gone
Her loving heart replaced with stone.
"See, the static means it's stuck!"
She feared it, he didn't give a fuck.
And there it was round and red
Fixed to the beam above his head.
She'd shuddered while he inflated it,
She'd pleaded, he'd refused to quit.
And as he rubbed it on his top
Her solitary tear had dropped.
He would continue, he would dictate
A coercive and illicit hate.
And all the while he failed to stop,
She prayed the bloody thing would pop.

Tish Camp

Her Alchemy

In an apothecary, at a ramshackle house, near water's edge,
where moonlight glistens, and toads are fouled,
on a dirt track road, a throat-calls at touch.

A woman sets to focus, hands in bowls,
pestle powdered beetle, with leaves of sweet juniper,
tied in muslin, pretty and foul,
words incantation, hand washed around,
till bowl-brimming, they fall,
black cat mewling, swallows all.

She strokes him, adjusts lit candles,
wipes hand on skirts, eyes are quick,
open-closed, mouth wanting,
stories from her oracle to sound.

She enchants, a love's devilry fix,
for fields of men, to plough hands,
imagined through her sky red hair.
Her gentle smile called to birds once,
but now a barren womb and fields call crows.

She Soothsays her life, with herbs in black,
this wife of sorcery, conjures up no trick,
her jinn, refuses to bring love back,
the pots spills, false hope in magic, washes away,
a silent heart and womb aches still.

Kayleigh Campbell

Eventide

When the day has succumbed
to the inevitability of night.

When Mayflies work,
frantic, hopeful in short lives.

When children resist lullabies,
when mothers hide in bathrooms.

When electricity flows
through the veins of the city.

When the tide is high
and waves crash before no-one.

When memories drift into rooms like ghosts,
haunting and welcome.

When eyes are heavy,
bodies yielding to time.

GPS Annual Open Poetry Competition 2019 ~ Winner

Contributors

Aidan Baker

Aidan Baker has worked as a librarian in Cambridge since 1982. His poetry publication record can be tracked via his blog
http://blurtmetry.blogspot.com
and his Twitter stream (**@AidanBaker**).

In 2017 he set himself the challenge of following the prompts in Jo Bell's book _52: write a poem a week. Start now. Keep going_ (Nine Arches Press, 2015), and 'Towel poem' is one of the products of that adventure.

Chris Barber

I have been writing poetry regularly for about ten years, at first submitting to a poetry page in The Citizen newspaper. At the suggestion and encouragement of the brilliant Samantha Pearse I started performing about four years ago. I have my own, closed, Facebook page, which includes my poems, musings on the absurdities of life, some short stories and plays.

Miriam Calleja

Miriam Calleja is the bilingual author of poetry collections *Pomegranate Heart* (EDE Books, 2015) and *Inside Skin* (a two-book series in collaboration with a lith photographer, EDE Books 2016).
She has also been published in international anthologies such as *For The Silent* (Indigo Dreams Publishing, 2019), *Persona Non Grata* (Fly on the Wall Press, 2018), *Leħen il-Malti* (Għadd 37, Għaqda tal-Malti, 2018), *Please Hear What I'm Not Saying* (editor Isabelle Kenyon, 2018), and *Poetic Potatoes* (a collaboration between Valletta 2018 and Inizjamed together with Leeuwarden, 2018) among others.

Her work has been translated into Slovene in the collection *Wara Settembru* (2018, Slovene Writers Association) and into Greek in the collection *Anthology of Young Maltese Poets* (Vakxikon, 2019).
She lives in Malta where she regularly facilitates creative writing workshops, literary salons, and poetry performances. She has read at events in Malta, Berlin, UK, Italy, San Francisco, and New York.
Miriam believes that poetry and prose are tools for storytelling that encourage unity. She has great faith in collaboration as a key to communication.
In 2015 she was shortlisted for a literary excellence award for her poem 'Burying the Dark', which has been published in an anthology by Magic Oxygen in the UK.
In 2017 she was recognised by the Network of Young Women Leaders as a leading female artist in Malta.
In 2018 she received an honourable mention for the national poetry competition Mons. Amante Buontempo.
In 2018 her poem was longlisted for the Troubadour International Prize.
www.miriamcalleja.com

Tish Camp

Tish Camp is a poet, writer and performer. Born in 60's London, of Trinidadian Irish heritage, her poetry embraces a wide range of issues including her working-class roots, politics, poverty, racial identity and feminist perspectives. Her work reflects observations on class, homelessness, homophobia, sexism, racism, sexuality, grief, loss and widowhood. Tish, founded Rise up Theatre, which seeks to empower communities through the arts. She instigated and co-ordinated 'The Search For Gloucestershire's Next Poet Laureate'. She conceived and curated the Soundbites Week Street Interviews on poetry across the county. Published in the Gloucestershire Poetry Society's 'V10 Pamphlet' and also their 2018 annual anthology 'Revolution', she can be found on social media at Facebook, Twitter, Instagram, Soundcloud and YouTube. Tish Camp has performed in Gloucestershire, throughout the South of England, London and as far as Barcelona. She will be looking to publish her own work in the near future.

https://www.facebook.com/ThisShiteGrief/
https://twitter.com/ThisShiteGrief
https://www.youtube.com/watch?v=wbJNH2p6QZo
https://www.instagram.com/writings_by_tish_camp/
https://soundcloud.com/gloucestershirepoet
http://www.tishcamp.co.uk

Kayleigh Campbell

Kayleigh Campbell is a PhD Researcher at Huddersfield University and she is an Editorial Assistant for Stand Magazine. She also works as a freelance proof-reader/editor.

She has been published in print and online, including Butcher's Dog, Black Bough Poetry and Riggwelter Press; she was also commended for the Geoff Stevens Prize. Her debut pamphlet, *Keepsake*, is available from Maytree Press.
Twitter - @kayyyleighc
Instagram - @kayleighhhc
Website - kayleighcampbell.co.uk

Jason Conway

Jason is an eco-poet, artist and designer based in Stroud, Gloucestershire. Drawing inspiration from life and the natural world, his mission is to encourage people to make a positive difference, protect nature, fight prejudice, face their fears and follow their dreams. Jason's debut collection 'Phoenix Rises' was published in 2018 and he has been published in The Blue Nib and Poetry Bus magazines.
www.facebook.com/jasonconwaypoetry
www.cre8urbrand.co.uk/jasonconwaypoetry

Z D Dicks

Z D Dicks is the Founder/CEO of the Gloucestershire Poetry Society and Gloucester Poetry Festival.

He holds an MA in Creative and Critical Writing. His work is concerned with the everyday and of the very serious business of living.

He has two books published by Black Eyes Publishing UK, Malcontent & Intimate Nature.
Blackeyespublishinguk.co.uk

María Castro Domínguez

Maria Castro Dominguez is the author of 'A Face in The Crowd', her 2016 Erbacce Press winning collection. Winner of the third prize in Brittle Star's Poetry Competition 2018 and finalist in Mslexia Max Poetry Competition. Joint first in the Orbis 185 Readers' Award 2019.

Her poems have appeared in *Obsessed With Pipework, Sarvasti, Apogee and Popshot Magazine*.

She has a Bachelor's degree in English philology and works as a translator and freelance writer.
Website: **mariacastrodominguez.com**

Twitter: **@marcasdom**
Instagram: afaceinthecrowdpoetry
Facebook: www.facebook.com/maria.c.dominguez.73

Tessa Foley

Tessa Foley is a writer from the south coast of the UK. Her work has been featured in numerous literary magazines including Agenda and the Fredericksburg Literary Art Review and she has been recognised in several competitions such as the Verve Poetry Competition and the Bristol Poetry Prize. Her debut poetry collection 'Chalet Between Thick Ears' was published by Live Canon and launched by Live Canon in November 2018
http://www.livecanon.co.uk/publications

She is now working on a one-woman poetry play.
www.tessafoley.com

Emily Hall (aged 9)
Emily Louise Anne Hall
9 years old
Born 27th July 2010

'I enjoy reading books and dancing. I like writing poems with my family. I hope to keep learning to write better and better poems in future.'

Sue Johnson
Sue Johnson is a poet, short story writer and novelist. Her work is inspired by country walks, fairy-tales and eavesdropping in cafes. Sue is a Writing Magazine Home Study Tutor. Follow her on Twitter @SueJohnson9. For more information about publications, workshops and critique service, see **www.writers-toolkit.co.uk**

Sue Kinsella
Sue hails from Dublin, Ireland. She has studied creative writing at NUI Maynooth. Her poems have appeared in the Blue Nib, Poetic Republic and Selfies and Portraits: Snapshots from the Library After Dark Writers Cafe.

Josephine Lay

'Josephine Lay is a published poet with two collections of poetry; Inside Reality and Unravelling, both published by 'Black Eyes'. Josephine is currently Poet in Residence at Cheltenham Library, and she is passionate about poetry and libraries, and the vital part they both play within community.

She is a member of The Gloucestershire Poetry Society and hosts 'Squawkers'; the monthly Poetry Night at The Sober Parrot, Cheltenham, under the GPS banner. She is a member of The Cheltenham Poetry Society and actively supports the Cheltenham Poetry Festival and the Gloucester Poetry Festival.

Lay's poems often speak of the human condition; of life, love, loss. Josephine is a firm believer that page poetry and performance poetry both play an important part in the modern-day poetry scene. She runs poetry workshops and performs her work in various venues around Gloucestershire, Wiltshire, and surrounding counties.'
Blackeyespublishinguk.co.uk

Peter Lay

Peter Lay has co-written a dual language (English/Chinese), cross cultural metaphorical conversation, 'Yellow Over the Mountain'.

He has always written poetry but since joining the Gloucestershire Poetry Society in early 2018 he has been performing in Gloucestershire, Wiltshire, Worcester, Birmingham & Stoke on Trent. He has visited Japan three times and during his trip last November he experienced an emotional event when in Nagasaki and Hiroshima. Several poems about this are featured in his new Poetry book, 'Still Tilting at Windmills' published by 'Black Eyes'.

Peter Lay ~ Performer, Poet & Publisher
Blackeyespublishinguk.co.uk

Charlie Markwick

Charlie Markwick is a Gloucester based professional storyteller and poet. He is a passionate advocate of the spoken word in all of its forms and believes in the power of words to transform lives. He is poet in residence at Gloucester Central Library. He played a major role in the recent search for the Gloucestershire Poet Laureate. As part of that campaign Charlie conducted the street-based interviews on the Soundbites Week.

Charlie recently published his first book "Orienteering", a collection of poetry that appears in his current show of the same name. Charlie is no stranger to the stage he's a long-time member of the Bristol Improv Theatre Unscripted Players.
http://charliem.poetrybooks.org/
https://soundcloud.com/gloucesterpoet
https://soundcloud.com/glospoetlaureate
http://www.yarnwhispering.co.uk/
https://www.facebook.com/OrienteeringTheatre

JLM Morton

JLM Morton grew up around these parts and is a poet, writer, mother, lover, friend,
thinker, doer, cold water addict.
www.jlmmorton.com

Patricia M Osborne

Patricia M Osborne is married with grown-up children and five grandchildren. She was born in Liverpool and now lives in West Sussex. In September 2018, Patricia finished an MA in Creative Writing with the University of Brighton and graduated with a Merit. She is a novelist, poet and short fiction writer. Her poems and short stories have been published in various literary magazines and anthologies and her first poetry pamphlet, Taxus Baccata, has been accepted for publication by Hedgehog Poetry Press. Her debut novel, *House of Grace, A Family Saga,* set in the 1950s/60s, was released in March 2017.

Patriciamosbornewriter.com

Facebook: Patricia M Osborne, Writer
Twitter: PMOsborneWriter

Clive Oseman

Clive Oseman is a Swindon based Brummie who has been performing on the spoken word scene since 2014. A multi slam winner who finished 6th at the Farrago UK slam finals in London this year, he mixes humorous and serious material and has featured or headlined at events in many towns and cities. His second collection, Life, was published in 2018, with a third expected in 2020.

He can be found on Facebook in his own name (personal account) or **@cliveosemanspokenword**, on Twitter **@Clive_Oseman** and Instagram **@Osemanclive**.

Carol Sheppard

Carol Sheppard is a poet and playwright who lives in the Forest of Dean which inspires much of her poetry. She has had poems published in several literary journals and exhibited in Biggar Poetry Garden. Her play The Drop of a Pin toured Gloucestershire in 2016. As well as poetry she has also had a short film and radio play produced and writes a weekly column in The Citizen newspaper. She is an active member of Dean Writers, PIPs Poetry Group, Gloucester Scriptorium Playwrights and Gloucestershire Poetry Society.

Laura Theis

Winner of the 2018 Hammond House Literary Prize for Poetry Shortlisted for the 2018 Yeovil Prize and the 2018 Live Canon Poetry Prize judged by Liz Berry.

Her poetry has previously appeared in various publications such as the London Reader, Strange Horizons and Rise Up Review.
http://lauratheis.weebly.com/

Susie Wilson

Susie Wilson has spent ten years teaching English to other people, whilst writing about them and life. Now she writes poetry, short stories and mildly disturbing Flash Fiction, whilst living in Sheffield and completing an MA in Creative Writing at The Writing School, Manchester Metropolitan University. She can be found on twitter **@concordmoose**

Thanks

Black Eyes Publishing UK for publishing this work.

Jason Conway of Cre8urbrand for the cover design.

Z D Dicks for poetry editing

The poets that successfully submitted their work for inclusion.

Any poets that were unsuccessful this time, we hope you come back stronger next time.

Zack Dicks for creating the GPS on 17th October 2016

The Fountain Inn, Gloucester for its continued support for our monthly, Villanelles event, hosted by Z D Dicks (Ziggy) & Jason Conway, held on the last Thursday of each month.

Waterstones Cafe, Gloucester for its continued support for our monthly, Poetry event, hosted by Sarah (Saffy) Snell-Pym & Tanya Feasey, held on the third Sunday of each month.

The Nelson Trust for its support over the last year for our monthly, Squawkers event, hosted by Josephine Lay, held every third Friday of each month at the Sober Parrot, Cheltenham.

All the amazing featured poets that have appeared at our events.

Everyone that ran a workshop for us.

All those that come to watch and listen, and those that take part via workshops and open mic at our events.

And especially our fantastic GPS members for making the society even greater in 2019

Finally, poetry is for everyone as life is poetry.

Special thanks to the following,

Z D Dicks
Jason Conway
Josephine Lay
Sarah 'Saffy' Snell-Pym
Tanya Feasey
Charlie Markwick
Tish Camp
Peter Lay
Clive Oseman & Nick Lovell (oooh Beehive)
Scott Cowley, James Osborn & Sue Hammond (Rusty Goat's Poetry Corner)
The Fountain Inn staff
Waterstones Café staff
The Sober Parrot Staff

THE GLOUCESTER POETRY FESTIVAL 2019

INTIMATE NATURE LAUNCH
MONDAY SEPT 30TH 7-10:30PM
THE FOUNTAIN INN GLOS

BARNIVERSE
THURSDAY OCT 3RD 7-10:00PM
TIGER'S EYE RESTAURANT GLOS

BARE WORDS
FRIDAY OCT 4TH 7-9PM
BAREWALL GALLERY STAFFS

GPS WATERSTONES
SUNDAY OCT 6TH 2-4 PM
WATERSTONES GLOS

BOOK WYRMS
WEDNESDAY OCT 9TH 2-4 PM
GLOUCESTER LIBRARY

HEADSPACE
THURSDAY OCT 10TH 7-10:00 PM
THE FOUNTAIN INN GLOS

BOOK WYRMS
WEDNESDAY OCT 16TH 2-4 PM
GLOUCESTER LIBRARY

PLATFORM ONE
WEDNESDAY OCT 16TH 7-10:00PM
THE STATION HOTEL GLOS

SQUAWKERS
FRIDAY OCT 18TH 7-10:30PM
THE SOBER PARROT CHELT

GPS WATERSTONES
SUNDAY OCT 20TH 2-4 PM
WATERSTONES GLOS

TO KNOW ME LAUNCH
SUNDAY OCT 20TH 4:45-7PM
ST MARY DE CRYPT CHURCH GLOS

PLATFORM TWO
THURSDAY OCT 24TH 7-10:00PM
THE STATION HOTEL GLOS

GORILLA SLAM
FRIDAY OCT 25TH 7-11:00PM
TIGER'S EYE RESTAURANT GLOS

ECHOES
SATURDAY OCT 26TH 7-10:00PM
FOLK MUSEUM GLOS

FOREST FINDS ITS VOICE
SUNDAY OCT 27TH 2:30-3:30PM
OLYMPUS THEATRE GLOS

VILLANELLES
SUNDAY OCT 27TH 7-10:30PM
THE FOUNTAIN INN GLOS

SORTILEGE
THURSDAY OCT 31ST 7-10:30PM
THE FOUNTAIN INN GLOS

FACEBOOK @GLOUCESTERPOETRYFESTIVAL
WWW.THEGLOUCESTERSHIREPOETRYSOCIETY.CO.UK

www.ingramcontent.com/pod-product-compliance
Lightning Source LLC
Chambersburg PA
CBHW071321080526
44587CB00018B/3313